Wars Waged Under the Microscope

The War Against Polio

Cynthia O'Brien

CRABTREE
PUBLISHING COMPANY
WWW.CRABTREEBOOKS.COM

CRABTREE
PUBLISHING COMPANY
WWW.CRABTREEBOOKS.COM

Author: Cynthia O'Brien

Editors: Sarah Eason, Jennifer Sanderson, and Ellen Rodger

Editorial director: Kathy Middleton

Design: Simon Borrough

Cover design and additional artwork: Katherine Berti

Photo research: Rachel Blount

Proofreader: Wendy Scavuzzo

Production coordinator and Prepress technician: Ken Wright

Print coordinator: Katherine Berti

Consultant: David Hawksett

Produced for Crabtree Publishing by Calcium Creative Ltd

Photo Credits

Cover: tl: CDC/Dr. Fred Murphy, Sylvia Whitfield, Wikimedia Commons; b: Yusnizam Yusof, Shutterstock; All other images Shutterstock

Inside: Alamy: Prisma Archivo: p. 6; Centers for Disease Control and Prevention: James Gathany: p. 25; Adam Hassan Haji, Kenya: p. 5; Mary Hilpertshauser: p. 19; Stacey Hoffman, M.P.H.: p. 14; Flickr: Conor Ashleigh for AusAID/Department of Foreign Affairs & Trade: p. 22; C.M. Schofield: p. 8; Shutterstock: Kwame Amo: p. 27; Davide Bonaldo: p. 4; FabrikaSimf: p. 15; Frank60: p. 24; Adam Gregor: p. 26; Illustration Forest: p. 13; Belen B Massieu: p. 17; Ninja SS: p. 12; Affendy Soeto: p. 11; A M Syed: p. 20; Vitstudio: p. 16; Wikimedia Commons: p. 7; Centers for Disease Control and Prevention: p. 21; City of Boston Archives: p. 18; New York World-Telegram and the Sun Newspaper Photograph Collection: p. 23; U.S. National Archives and Records Administration: p. 10; Works Progress Administration, Library of Congress: p. 9.

Library and Archives Canada Cataloguing in Publication

Title: The war against polio / Cynthia O'Brien.
Names: O'Brien, Cynthia (Cynthia J.), author.
Description: Series statement: Wars waged under the microscope | Includes bibliographical references and index.
Identifiers: Canadiana (print) 20210189053 | Canadiana (ebook) 20210189061 | ISBN 9781427151315 (hardcover) | ISBN 9781427151391 (softcover) | ISBN 9781427151476 (HTML) | ISBN 9781427151551 (EPUB)
Subjects: LCSH: Poliomyelitis—Juvenile literature. | LCSH: Poliomyelitis—Treatment—Juvenile literature. | LCSH: Poliomyelitis—Prevention—Juvenile literature. | LCSH: Epidemics—Juvenile literature.
Classification: LCC RC180.2 .O27 2022 | DDC j614.5/49—dc23

Library of Congress Cataloging-in-Publication Data

Names: O'Brien, Cynthia (Cynthia J.) author.
Title: The war against polio / Cynthia O'Brien.
Description: New York, NY : Crabtree Publishing Company, [2022] | Series: Wars waged under the microscope | Includes index.
Identifiers: LCCN 2021016654 (print) | LCCN 2021016655 (ebook) | ISBN 9781427151315 (hardcover) | ISBN 9781427151391 (paperback) | ISBN 9781427151476 (ebook) | ISBN 9781427151551 (epub)
Subjects: LCSH: Poliomyelitis--Juvenile literature. | Poliomyelitis--Treatment--Juvenile literature. | Poliomyelitis--Prevention--Juvenile literature. | Epidemics--Juvenile literature.
Classification: LCC RC180.2 .O27 2022 (print) | LCC RC180.2 (ebook) | DDC 614.5/49--dc23
LC record available at https://lccn.loc.gov/2021016654
LC ebook record available at https://lccn.loc.gov/2021016655

Crabtree Publishing Company
www.crabtreebooks.com   1-800-387-7650

Printed in the U.S.A./062021/CG20210401

Published in Canada
Crabtree Publishing
616 Welland Ave.
St. Catharines, Ontario
L2M 5V6

Published in the United States
Crabtree Publishing
347 Fifth Ave.
Suite 1402-145
New York, NY 10016

Contents

The Enemy

Poliomyelitis, or polio, is a serious, sometimes deadly, disease. It is caused by a virus—a tiny organism too small to be seen by the naked eye. There is no cure for polio, but it can be prevented. Although most of the world is now free of polio, in some countries, the battle to control the disease continues.

The poliovirus can affect anyone, but children who are under five years old are most at risk. This is because young children are less likely to wash their hands properly. Handwashing is especially important after going to the toilet and before eating.

Infected by Polio

The poliovirus infects people's throats and **intestines**. It is very contagious, which means it spreads easily from person to person.

Many people have no symptoms, or signs of sickness, and do not know they have been infected with polio. Most often, the virus spreads when people come in contact with infected people's feces, or waste. For example, the infected feces can **contaminate** water that other people use. Sometimes, the virus can spread in droplets from an infected person's sneeze or cough.

Polio, an Ancient Problem

Polio has been a problem for thousands of years—the first recorded cases of it date back to ancient Egyptian times. It is only in very recent times that people have been able to fight back against the disease with **vaccines**, which have drastically reduced polio **outbreaks** around the world.

These Kenyan children hold up their fingers, which are marked with a color to show they have been vaccinated against polio.

The last case of polio in the United States was reported in 1979. Canada's last case was in 1977. The **World Health Organization (WHO)** declared the Americas polio-free in 1994. In August 2020, Nigeria became the latest country to be declared free of polio. However, Pakistan and Afghanistan are still fighting the disease. As long as cases of polio exist, there is a threat that the virus will spread and create new outbreaks. That is why scientists around the world are working hard to take the fight to this life-changing disease and wipe it out forever.

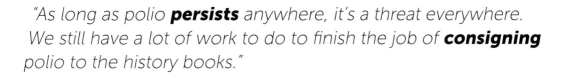

*"As long as polio **persists** anywhere, it's a threat everywhere. We still have a lot of work to do to finish the job of **consigning** polio to the history books."*

Tedros Adhanom Ghebreyesus, Director-General, WHO, 2020

The Battle Begins

For centuries, people suffered from devastating **paralysis** or death caused by polio, but they did not know how to treat the disease. From 1800 to the mid-1900s, polio **epidemics** in Europe and North America caused widespread fear. Scientists around the world worked to find a way to fight the disease.

This image from ancient Egypt shows a man using a crutch to help him walk. His **disability** was likely caused by polio.

First Discoveries

In the mid-1800s, a German scientist named Jakob von Heine discovered that polio was different from other diseases that caused paralysis. Then, during a polio outbreak in Sweden in 1887, Karl Medin studied the differences in cases. Medin reported that patients who suffered **fevers** at two different stages were paralyzed after the second fever. Medin reasoned that the **central nervous system** was affected at this stage, and that led to paralysis.

Still, no one knew what caused polio until 1908, when Austrian scientists Karl Landsteiner and Erwin Popper proved that a virus causes the disease. Researchers began their studies into the virus as outbreaks of polio continued. By 1949, scientists identified the three types of polioviruses. This was a very important finding because any effective vaccine would have to work on all three types.

A Public Panic

Meanwhile, frightened parents blamed insects, **imported** food, swimming pools, and many other things for infecting their children. Nothing stopped the outbreaks, and thousands of people became sick each year. **Sanitation** improved in many areas, but polio outbreaks increased. One idea is that this happened because the cleaner conditions kept babies from becoming infected with poliovirus, so they did not develop **immunity** to it. Babies still had some immunity to the virus, passed on by their mothers. So if they caught the virus, they often did not even seem to be sick. When uninfected babies grew into older children or adults, then were exposed to the virus, they could become very sick.

Ivar Wickman carried out experiments during a polio outbreak in Sweden in 1905. Wickman discovered that people could be infected by polio and spread it, despite having no symptoms, or signs of illness.

UNDER THE MICROSCOPE

Landsteiner and Popper conducted their experiments during a polio epidemic in Vienna, Austria. They collected a **sample** from the **spinal cord** of a boy who had died of polio. They infected monkeys with the sample, and the monkeys developed the same disease. They went on to find the virus in other **tissues** in the throat and intestines.

Polio Attacks

From the late 1800s, polio outbreaks struck regularly in summer months. This may have happened because the poliovirus spreads more easily in warmer weather. But some years were worse than others.

Dealing with an Epidemic

The first large polio epidemic in the United States happened in 1916. By that time, scientists knew that the poliovirus caused the disease, but there seemed no way to prevent it. That year, more than 27,000 people in the country contracted the virus, and 6,000 died.

Across the United States, people tried to find ways to keep themselves and their children safe. Some towns started banning events and making it illegal to travel from one place to another. Armed policemen patrolled the roads as well as bus and train stations. If someone became sick with polio, they had to **quarantine** at home. Polio patients in the hospitals were kept apart from all other patients. Today, these methods are still used to try to keep viruses from spreading.

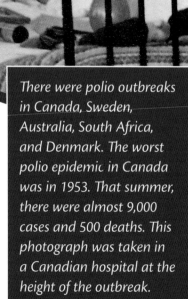

There were polio outbreaks in Canada, Sweden, Australia, South Africa, and Denmark. The worst polio epidemic in Canada was in 1953. That summer, there were almost 9,000 cases and 500 deaths. This photograph was taken in a Canadian hospital at the height of the outbreak.

CASE STUDY: ROOSEVELT AND THE MARCH OF DIMES

The polio epidemics in the United States affected many thousands of people. One of them was Franklin Delano Roosevelt. In 1921, Roosevelt became paralyzed after a suspected poliovirus infection at the age of 39. Twelve years later, he became president of the United States. Polio outbreaks were still happening every year, so as president, Roosevelt held yearly fundraising events to raise money for research.

In 1938, Roosevelt founded the National Foundation for Infantile Paralysis (NFIP). The foundation's aim was to support polio research and treatment for people who were affected. It asked people, including children, to donate whatever they could afford, even if it was just a dime. Volunteers across the country went door to door to collect money in what was known as the "March of Dimes."

Every January, across the United States, Birthday Balls for President Roosevelt's birthday were held. These helped raise money to fight polio.

By the end of the first month, the March of Dimes collected 2,680,000 dimes, or $268,000. That is the same as raising almost $5,000,000 in 2020. The NFIP was able to fund medical research and help patients pay for treatments. The research led to the first polio vaccines and a huge victory in the war against polio.

Creating a Defense

As epidemics of polio ravaged countries, scientists studied the virus to better understand how it attacked the human body and to find ways to stop it. Creating a vaccine became a top priority.

Making a Vaccine

The first polio vaccines, created in the 1930s, were disasters. Tests on about 10,000 children resulted in several infections and deaths. Then, in 1947, when Dr. Jonas Salk was the director of the Virus Research Laboratory in Pittsburgh, Pennsylvania, the NFIP funded his research. Salk developed a vaccine using inactive, or killed, poliovirus Types 1, 2, and 3. In 1955, the vaccine was approved for use.

Meanwhile, Dr. Albert Sabin was also researching the poliovirus. Sabin used a weakened, but still active, virus for his vaccine. The vaccine was approved in 1961. It was cheaper to produce and easier to give to people as it needed two drops in the mouth instead of an injection. From 1963 to 1999, Sabin's oral polio vaccine was used all over the world.

The Polio Hall of Fame opened in 1958. The sculptures on the wall honor Salk, Sabin, and others who fought against polio.

CASE STUDY:
THE CUTTER INCIDENT

In spring 1955, a widespread vaccination program began. Thousands of children across the United States and Canada received the new Salk vaccine. Salk supplied 55 pages of instructions to the laboratories producing the doses. However, there was no strict monitoring of the process once it began.

In the Western and Midwestern United States, more than 200,000 children received the Salk polio vaccine. Not long afterward, about 40,000 children became sick with polio. The outbreak left 200 patients paralyzed and 10 dead. The cause of the outbreak was traced back to vaccines made by the Cutter Laboratories, a company in California. An investigation uncovered the mistake. The Cutter Labs had not inactivated poliovirus Type 1 properly. The Cutter vaccine was taken off the market.

Countries such as Indonesia still use a version of the Sabin vaccine. Since 2000, children in the United States receive a version of the Salk vaccine.

The "Cutter Incident" led to a distrust of the Salk vaccine and a switch to the Sabin vaccine, when it became available. However, small changes in producing the Salk vaccine made it safer and more effective, and it was used again starting in the 1980s.

An Invisible Threat

Viruses are **microbes** that are so tiny they can only be seen with a **microscope**. Microbes are everywhere in the world, including the soil, water, plants, and the human body. Most of them are harmless, but some can be deadly.

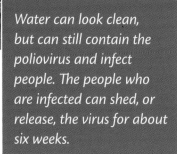

Disease-Causing Pathogens

Pathogens are microbes that cause diseases. Some viruses are pathogens. In the wild and in laboratories, scientists look at where pathogens are found and how they behave. This research helps find ways to wage war on these tiny enemies.

Water can look clean, but can still contain the poliovirus and infect people. The people who are infected can shed, or release, the virus for about six weeks.

Pathogens enter the body in different ways. They also affect different parts of the body and can move around through the body's systems. Pathogens often spread easily, such as from person to person if an infected person coughs or sneezes. They may stay active on surfaces that people touch or infect food that they eat. Once inside the body, pathogens wage war on healthy **cells**.

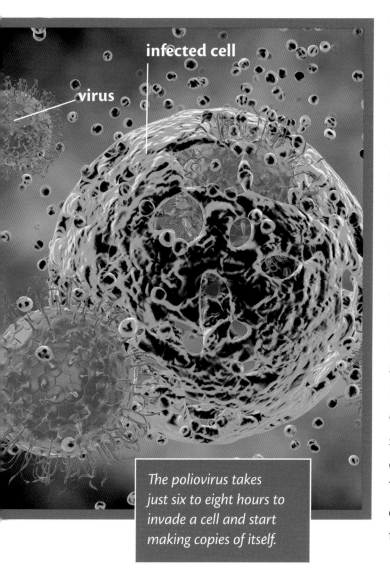

infected cell

virus

The poliovirus takes just six to eight hours to invade a cell and start making copies of itself.

Viruses—Small but Deadly

Scientists have identified more than 200 viruses that make people sick. Viruses come in different shapes and sizes, but they all have something in common: They cannot replicate, or make copies of themselves, on their own. To replicate, they need to invade living cells in plants, animals, or **bacteria**. Different viruses target different cells in the body. For example, the poliovirus first attacks the cells in the throat before moving on. Once inside a cell, the virus takes over. The virus sends chemical messages to the cell, telling it to replicate the virus. The virus copies break out of the cells and invade other cells. Then the process starts again.

UNDER THE MICROSCOPE

The body's immune system helps defend against infections. The system is made up of **organs**, cells, and **proteins** that work together. For example, some white blood cells seek out and kill invading pathogens. Others produce **antibodies**, or proteins that bind to invading pathogens and stop them from attacking healthy cells and replicating.

Under Attack

The poliovirus enters the body through the mouth. It usually spreads through water, food, or hands that are contaminated with feces containing the virus. In the worst cases, polio attacks and destroys the body's motor neuron cells. These cells control muscle movement, from walking to swallowing and breathing.

First Symptoms

Polio can be difficult to spot because about 90 percent of people have no symptoms. Even so, these people are still infectious and may pass the virus onto other people without knowing. People have different reactions, depending on their immune systems and other health issues. So, a person with no symptoms could infect another person who could become very sick.

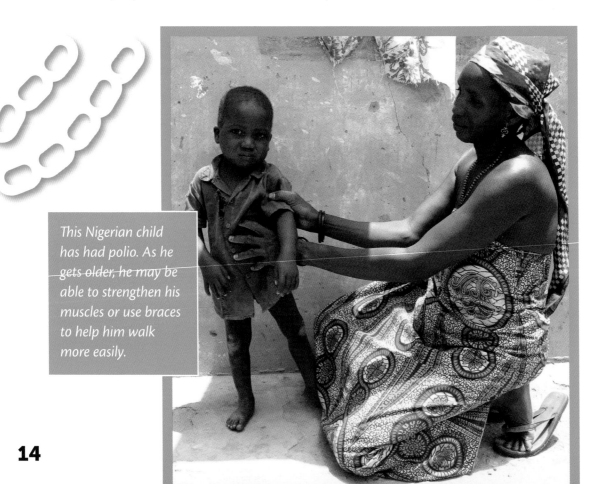

This Nigerian child has had polio. As he gets older, he may be able to strengthen his muscles or use braces to help him walk more easily.

A person with symptoms usually has a sore throat, mild fever, and a headache. They may also feel very tired and have an upset stomach. Polio symptoms appear as the virus starts to replicate, or make copies of itself, in the gastrointestinal tract. This is a series of organs, including the mouth and stomach, that are joined by a long tube and are responsible for processing food. These symptoms can last about 2 to 5 days, then go away without treatment.

When Polio Becomes Serious

About a week or two after a person becomes infected, the poliovirus can infect the nerve cells in the spinal cord or the brain. If it does, patients usually develop severe muscle pain. Less than 1 percent of the time, a poliovirus infection develops into poliomyelitis, which causes paralysis. Paralysis can happen quickly and can be permanent. It usually affects the legs more than the arms. Some people may get some or all of their movement back. In the worst cases, the chest and throat muscles stop working, and patients have trouble breathing and swallowing. This is called bulbar polio, which can be deadly.

A blood test can detect if there are any antibodies for the poliovirus. If antibodies are present, the person has had the poliovirus at some point.

Studying the Enemy

Over the years, scientists have worked to understand and battle the poliovirus. In the past and today, researchers look closely at how the virus attacks and its effects on the body. Looking at the poliovirus can also help scientists understand how other viruses work.

The Poliovirus at Work

The poliovirus is a human enterovirus. There are many types of enteroviruses, and most of them cause only mild symptoms, such as fever. The poliovirus is dangerous because it can go on to infect the body's central nervous system. Enteroviruses usually infect the intestines and **transmit** through feces. Once inside the intestines, the poliovirus attaches to receptors, or proteins, on the surface of a cell. This "unlocks" the cell so the virus can get in. Within about six to eight hours, the poliovirus can make between 10,000 and 100,000 copies of itself. These copies break out of the cell and go into the bloodstream. The poliovirus can then infect the central nervous system.

*The poliovirus is tiny and simple. About one in every 200 poliovirus **particles** will be able to infect a single cell at any one time.*

Old and New Polio

Wild poliovirus is the virus found naturally in the environment. There are three types of wild poliovirus: Type 1, Type 2, and Type 3. Today, only poliovirus Type 1 exists. However, wild polio is not the only problem—there can also be issues with infection from **vaccine-derived polioviruses (VDPVs)**. Those are weakened polioviruses that were originally included in an oral polio vaccine.

VDPVs threaten communities in some countries where few people have been **immunized** against polio. The longer a VDPV spreads, the more it changes. The risk is that the virus will turn into a form called a circulating vaccine-derived poliovirus (cVDPV), meaning the virus spreads in the community. That can cause paralysis.

Bringing in Polio

Thankfully, outbreaks of cVDPV are rare. Countries that have eradicated, or gotten rid of, poliovirus have the risk of cases from an imported virus. The virus enters these countries with travelers from where polio is still active. The last case of imported polio in the United States was reported in 1993.

VDPVs can be devastating in areas were there is little immunity against polio. The paralysis caused by polio leads to muscle atrophy, or very weak muscles, from lack of use. As children recover from the virus and grow, their legs may not grow normally.

Armed with Medicine

There is no cure for polio and no medicine that kills the poliovirus once people become infected. Doctors can only treat the symptoms. Since 1955, vaccines have provided the best defense against the disease.

Early Treatments

In the 1800s and early 1900s, little was known about polio. Doctors tried many treatments, including injecting patients with medications used for other diseases. Even if patients recovered, many still had trouble breathing. One treatment was to lay patients in rocking beds. As the top of the bed went up, it helped draw air into the lungs. As the bed went down, the movement helped push out air. In the 1900s, devices called "iron lungs" helped people breathe.

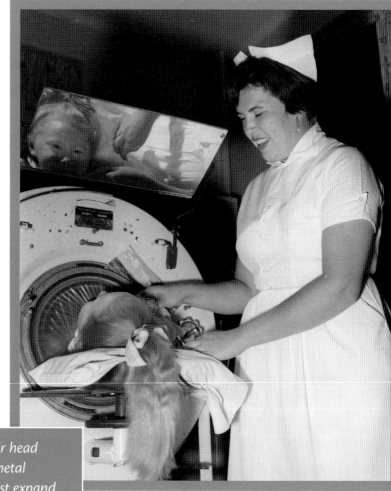

A patient lay in an iron lung, with their head exposed. Air was pumped out of the metal cylinder, which made the patient's chest expand. This drew air into the patient's nose or mouth.

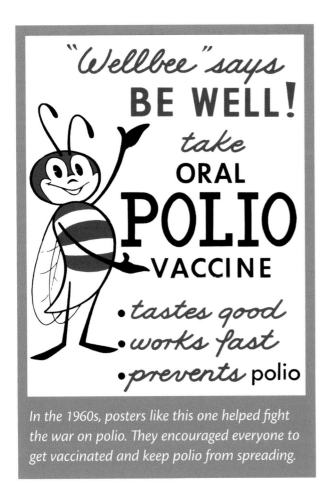

"Wellbee" says
BE WELL!
take
ORAL
POLIO
VACCINE

• *tastes good*
• *works fast*
• *prevents* polio

In the 1960s, posters like this one helped fight the war on polio. They encouraged everyone to get vaccinated and keep polio from spreading.

New Therapies

In the 1930s, Elizabeth Kenny, a nurse from Australia, began treating polio patients. She applied hot, damp packs to the body to ease muscle pain. She also massaged the muscles and exercised the limbs. In 1942, she founded the Sister Kenny **Rehabilitation** Institute in the United States. Hospitals across the country began using the "Kenny Method." Today, people use similar methods to help polio patients. Modern medicines can relieve pain and fever in milder cases of polio. In severe cases, patients who cannot breathe well may have to use **ventilators**. These are machines that move air in and out of the lungs.

UNDER THE MICROSCOPE

The Poliovirus Antiviral Initiative (PAI) sponsors the development of new medications for polio. Antivirals help stop viruses from reproducing, or copying themselves, inside the body. Two polio antivirals are in **clinical studies** and showing good results. Both antivirals target VDPVs, the cause of the most outbreaks.

Taking It to the Front Line

Every year, millions of children are given the polio vaccine. In countries such as the United States, children have four doses of the vaccine between the ages of two months and six years old. If enough children are vaccinated in a region, the virus dies out there.

War and Poverty Zones

In developing countries and war zones, vaccination programs are more difficult to run. It can be hard to get medicines to people living in war-torn countries or crowded **refugee** camps. Others may live in deserts, mountainous regions, or other areas that are difficult to reach. There are other challenges, too. Some people do not have good information about the cause of polio or how vaccines can help. They worry that the vaccine will harm their children. Many refuse to have their children vaccinated.

By the 2000s, organizations had helped eradicate polio in most countries. Some of the most important groups in this fight were the Global Polio Eradication Initiative (GPEI),

About 86 percent of the children around the world received three doses of the polio vaccine in 2019. People use donkeys, motorcycles, or helicopters to carry vaccines to remote places or war zones.

END POLIO NOW

Rotary Club International, the Bill & Melinda Gates Foundation, and the United Nations Children's Fund (UNICEF). Despite their efforts, outbreaks continued, particularly in Nigeria, Afghanistan, India, and Pakistan. The organizations had to find a way to reach **rural** areas and convince the people to accept the vaccinations.

Social Mobilizers

Thousands of local people, mostly women, became "social mobilizers." Trained social mobilizers are links between families and the health clinics or health care workers that give the vaccines. Having women take on this work made it easier to talk to mothers who were more comfortable with female visitors. Also, some cultural traditions have restrictions on the contact between women and men. Female social mobilizers are allowed to visit women in their homes.

Community workers in Pakistan go door to door to teach people about the polio vaccine and encourage parents to have their children immunized.

"*The more time you can spend getting your shoes dusty walking and working together in the field, the better you will understand the challenges.*"

Dr. Sue Gerber, *epidemiologist*, Bill & Melinda Gates Foundation

Surviving Polio

Most polio patients do not have lasting problems. But for some, polio leaves them with breathing problems, brain damage, or paralysis. Dealing with these issues can be even more difficult if healthcare is not easy to access.

Learning to Move Again

When people are recovering from a polio infection, their legs, arms, or other parts of the body can feel very weak and painful. Physiotherapy includes exercises that strengthen the muscles. Many polio survivors need devices to support their legs or other parts of the body that have been affected. Some people with weakened chest and stomach muscles may need a small ventilator to help them breathe properly, especially at night. Others with severe paralysis may have to use a wheelchair or wear artificial limbs. Many others rely on devices such as canes and leg braces. Early braces were made of metal with leather straps. Some had special shoes attached. Those devices were helpful, but very heavy. Modern materials offer strong support, and are much lighter.

Using bars for support, this post-polio patient exercises her leg muscles during a rehabilitation session.

CASE STUDY:
POST-POLIO SYNDROME

For millions of people who have had polio, there is another threat to their health. Post-polio syndrome (PPS) strikes as many as 40 years after people have fully recovered from polio. People with this condition find that muscles that were affected the first time, start to weaken and become very painful again. Other muscles also become weak. Patients feel extremely tired and have trouble breathing. Other issues, such as scoliosis, or curvature of the spine, can add to the pain.

PPS is not contagious and is not caused by a new poliovirus infection. It usually strikes people who have had a severe case of the disease. Polio destroys nerve cells, but as people recover, the cells find muscle fibers that still work, and people are able to move better. Scientists do not know what causes PPS, but it may be related to overworking muscles, joints, and the surviving nerve cells. After years without any braces, wheelchairs, or other devices, people may have to start using them again. Physiotherapy can help improve the strength in the muscles, but sometimes damage is permanent.

Most polio survivors go on to lead full, active lives. Wilma Rudolph (shown here) overcame paralysis to compete in the 1956 and 1960 Olympics.

While there is no cure for PPS, organizations such as Post-Polio Health International (PHI) help fund scientific research into it.

New Weapons

Organizations such as GPEI are helping fight the war on polio. They sponsor scientific research and help ensure that vaccines are produced and are available wherever they are needed.

Who Is Involved?

In 1979, volunteers from the Rotary Club helped immunize 6 million children in the Philippines. The Club then became a founding member of the GPEI. Organizations such as this are crucial because they raise money to pay for the work of research scientists, doctors, nurses, community workers, and more. They raise awareness and recruit volunteers. There is also a continuing need to make sure there are enough vaccine doses for every child.

The GPEI hopes that widespread vaccination programs will protect every child and help win the war on polio within the next few years.

Programs That Work

World statistics show that vaccination programs brought cases of wild poliovirus down by 99 percent since 1988. Most programs immunize children with oral polio vaccine, but the aim is to replace these with injected polio vaccine. This is happening slowly.

Scientists are working on ways to make vaccination easier. For example, current vaccines must be kept cold before they can be delivered to patients. This can present problems in many areas where access to refrigerators is difficult. Scientists are developing an injected polio vaccine that does not have to be kept cold. A vaccine like that would be easier to transport and keep in hot countries and in places without refrigerators.

There are also new studies on how the brain "rewires" itself after a virus attack. Understanding how these changes happen will help scientists develop better treatments for polio and other diseases that affect the nervous system.

UNDER THE MICROSCOPE

Scientists are looking at ways to make the oral polio vaccine safer. This involves finding ways to stop VDPVs from changing and causing disease. Once a new oral polio vaccine is available, it could be the easiest way to stop outbreaks of VDPVs.

A promising new vaccine uses poliovirus particles that have been changed so they cannot replicate. If successful, the vaccine would be cheaper to make, and it would not cause polio outbreaks.

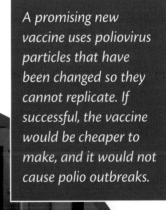

Future Warfare

In 2015, the WHO declared that the wild poliovirus Type 2 was eradicated around the world. Four years later, the world was free of Type 3. These great achievements are the result of many years of work by scientists, health professionals, volunteers, and others. But the battle against polio does not stop there.

*Teams of people cover up in protective clothing to collect water and **sewage** samples. At the lab, scientists test for VDPV and wild poliovirus.*

Polio Detectives

Keeping track of the poliovirus can be difficult. People cross the borders to and from countries where polio is still present. Every day, thousands of health care workers vaccinate children at border crossing points in Pakistan and Afghanistan. They also look for signs of illness in the children passing through.

Since many people have no symptoms, it is important to find where the virus may be hiding. To do this, scientists conduct environmental surveillance. This means looking for clues in the local water, and especially community sewage. These tests will show if the virus is circulating in the area. Finding this information early can help protect others.

New Enemies

The campaign against the poliovirus was going full speed ahead until another threat stopped it: COVID-19. The **pandemic** that began in 2020 shifted the focus away from polio vaccinations to treating COVID-19 patients and developing a vaccine for this new virus. Many health care workers, including the social mobilizers, began working to fight COVID-19 at the same time as trying to continue the battle against polio. They brought people information about both diseases and identified cases.

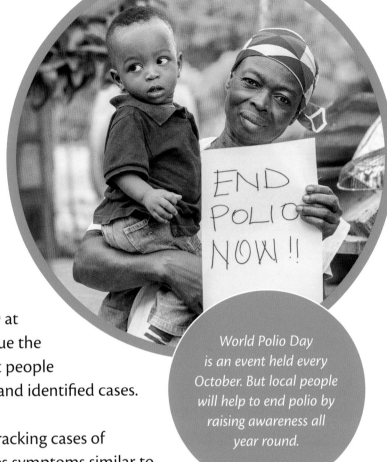

World Polio Day is an event held every October. But local people will help to end polio by raising awareness all year round.

Since 2014, scientists have been tracking cases of another serious disease that shares symptoms similar to polio. Acute flaccid myelitis (AFM), has similar symptoms to polio and also tends to affect young children. People with AFM experience sudden weakness or paralysis. They may have flu-like symptoms and some trouble breathing. Those symptoms seem to point to a viral infection. By testing patients' spinal fluid, researchers discovered the disease was linked to enteroviruses.

• •

"The eradication of wild polio virus Type 3 is a major milestone towards a polio-free world, but we cannot relax."

Matshidiso Moeti, Regional Director for Africa, WHO

• •

Timeline

People have been battling polio for thousands of years. Slowly, science is winning the war against this devastating disease.

1350–580 BCE   Ancient Egyptian images show paralysis, possibly from poliomyelitis.

1789   Dr. Michael Underwood writes the first medical description of polio.

1840   Jakob von Heine reports that polio involves the spinal cord.

1843   The first cases of polio are reported in the United States.

1894   First epidemic in the United States occurs in Vermont. There are at least 123 cases, with 18 people dead and 50 people left paralyzed. Most were children under six years old.

1905   Swedish doctor Ivar Wickman observes that polio is a contagious disease after a reported 1,200 cases.

1908   Karl Landsteiner discovers that the poliovirus causes polio.

1916   A polio outbreak in the United States kills about 6,000 people.

1928   Philip Drinker and Louis Agassiz Shaw develop the iron lung.

1935 The first polio vaccine trials fail.

1949 John Enders, a microbiologist, grows the poliovirus in different tissue cultures, paving the way for Salk's vaccine.

1952 More than 58,000 cases of polio are recorded in the United States.

1954 John Enders, Thomas Weller, and Frederick Robbins win the Nobel Prize in Physiology or Medicine for their work on the poliovirus.

1955 Jonas Salk's polio vaccine is declared safe and effective.

1961 Albert Sabin develops the oral polio vaccine.

1979 The last case in the United States caused by wild poliovirus is recorded.

1985 Rotary International launches PolioPlus program.

1988 Rotary Club International , UNICEF, and the WHO announce the GPEI and plan to eliminate polio by 2000. At the time, 25 countries report cases of poliomyelitis, with about 350,000 cases altogether.

1994 All of the Americas are declared polio-free.

2000 550 million children receive the polio vaccine. The Western Pacific, including Australia and China, is declared polio-free.

2006 Wild poliovirus remains in just four countries: Afghanistan, India, Nigeria, and Pakistan.

2012 The last case of Type 3 poliovirus is reported.

2014 India is declared polio-free.

2015 The WHO declares Type 2 poliovirus eradicated.

2018 Polio infections are down by 99 percent since 1988, with only 33 reported cases from the wild poliovirus.

2020 Nigeria is declared polio free.

Glossary

antibodies Substances produced by the body that fight off invading bacteria and viruses

bacteria Single-celled organisms that can cause disease

cells Units that make up all living things

central nervous system The parts of the body, including the brain and the spinal cord, that control movement and other functions

clinical studies Research to discover more about a disease and its treatment

consigning Delivering

contaminate To make dirty or to infect

disability A problem with the body that affects a person's movement or functions

epidemic Situations in which thousands of people in a community or country catch a disease at the same time

epidemiologist A scientist who studies how diseases start and spread, and how to control them

fevers High body temperatures

immunity A body's ability to stop a disease from affecting it

immunized Given a vaccine to provide immunity, or protection against disease

imported Brought in from another country

intestines Long tubes in the body that help digest food

microbes Tiny living things, including bacteria and viruses

microscope An instrument that uses special lenses to magnify, or make very small things large enough to see

organism A living thing

organs Parts of the body, such as the heart and lungs, that have specific functions

outbreaks Infections of more than one person

pandemic A situation in which a disease spreads and affects people across the world

paralysis Inability to move all or part of the body

particles Tiny pieces of something

persists Continues

proteins The substances that do most of the work in cells

quarantine A period of time when people with a disease, or suspected of having a disease, are kept away from other people

refugee A person who has been forced to leave their country to escape war, persecution, or natural disaster

rehabilitation The process of making a person well again

rural Not in the city or a built-up area

sample A small amount of something, such as blood, for testing

sanitation Providing clean drinking water and sewage removal

sewage Human waste such as urine and feces

spinal cord A series of nerves that run down the center of the back and carry messages between the brain and the rest of the body

tissues Groups of similar cells, forming muscles, skin, or fat

transmit Spread from one person to another

vaccine-derived polioviruses (VDPVs) A virus that was originally part of a poliovirus vaccine but has changed over time and become like wild polio

vaccines Substances that help protect against certain diseases

ventilators Machines that help people breathe, or breathe for them

virus A microscopic organism that can cause sickness

World Health Organization (WHO) An organization that helps governments improve their health services

Learning More

Find out more about polio and how the war against this disease is being won.

Books

Baum, Margaux, and Natalie Goldstein. *Viruses* (Germs: Disease-Causing Organisms). Rosen Central, 2016.

Brundle, Joanna. *Vaccines* (Life-Saving Science). Enslow, 2020.

Close, Edward. *Germ Warfare* (Discovery Education: How It Works). PowerKids Press, 2014.

Harris, Duchess, and Heather Hudak. *The Discovery of the Polio Vaccine* (Perspectives on American Progress). Core Library, 2018.

Websites

Find a basic explanation of polio at:
https://kids.britannica.com/kids/article/polio/390972

Follow an interactive timeline to discover the story of polio at:
https://polioeradication.org/polio-today/history-of-polio

Watch a video that explains how vaccine-derived polio can spread at:
https://polioeradication.org/polio-today/polio-prevention/the-virus/vaccine-derived-polio-viruses

Learn more about Jonas Salk at:
https://youngzine.org/news/societyarts/thank-you-dr-jonas-salk

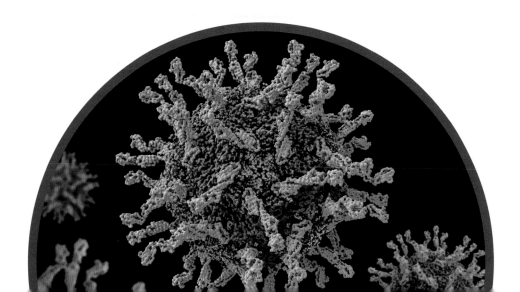

Index

A B O U T   T H E   A U T H O R

Cynthia O'Brien has written many books for children, including books about science and how the body works. Researching this book, she learned a lot about polio and the work that microbiologists and others are doing in the fight against it.